FEASTING

A CELEBRATION OF FOOD IN ART

PAINTINGS FROM
THE ART INSTITUTE
OF CHICAGO

JAMES YOOD

UNIVERSE

FEASTING
A CELEBRATION OF FOOD IN ART

Overleaf:

IGNACE HENRI JEAN THEODORE
FANTIN-LATOUR

French (1836-1904)
Still Life: Corner of a Table, 1873
Oil on canvas; $37^{15}/_{16}$ x $49^{3}/_{16}$ in.
Ada Turnball Hertle Fund (1951.226)

Published in the
United States of America
in 1992 by
UNIVERSE
300 Park Avenue South
New York, NY 10010

Library of Congress Cataloging-in-Publication Data

Yood, James.
    Feasting: a celebration of food in art/James
    W. Yood; in association with The Art
    Institute of Chicago.
            p.   cm.
    ISBN 0-87663-646-6
    1. Still-life painting. 2. Food in art.
    3. Dinners and dining in art.
    I. Art Institute of Chicago.   II. Title
ND1390.Y66   1992   92-14004
758'.9641—dc20   CIP

92 93 94 95 / 10 9 8 7 6 5 4 3 2 1

Printed in Singapore

Cover and Book Design: Christina B. Bliss

TABLE OF
CONTENTS

A NOURISHMENT OF TASTE

⚊ BY ⚊
JAMES YOOD

First we cry, then we eat. And eat and eat and eat; from birth until death, this fundamental activity continues, in an unending and infinitely variable chain of ingestion and digestion. Biologically, food nourishes us, providing the fuel for life. The drive to eat is instinctual for the infant, but as the child grows, he or she develops individual tastes, and the activity of eating takes on new, increasingly complex meanings. The average adult consumes approximately one ton of food and drink each and every year. Although as necessary to human survival as breathing, eating differs from respiration in that it is a conscious and, in most instances, a controlled activity, an ordered system within which we manifest many of our desires and aspirations—both as individuals with idiosyncratic tastes and as participants in a larger culture. The biological

requirements that eating satisfies are only the opening salvo, the chemical background, for the complex role that food plays in helping us define some primal elements in the human condition.

The old adage says it best: "All animals eat, but only humans dine." Just as architecture makes a cultural construct out of our need for shelter, the communal meal provides social as well as physical nourishment. Eating is intertwined with almost every aspect of our existence, from religious practices to psychological principles of self-definition. It can be a vehicle of desire, sensuality, greed, solace, punishment, obeisance, self-love, or self-hate; it can exalt or degrade, enrich or debase.

Throughout history, cultures have invested the rituals of sustenance with heavy layers of symbolism. Celebrations and customs centered around the meal define us as social beings, and food, in the social context, can broaden and deepen the texture of our relationships with family, lover, or friend. We break bread to denote our commonality, our shared condition as beings with multiple appetites, many of which can be well satisfied at the table. The very phrase, "breaking bread," is a metaphor for coming together, meaning far more than simply the portioning out of food; to share a meal is among the most basic, universal ways of showing good will.

If we do not eat, we die. Historically, it was probably the need to secure dependable and renewable food sources that led humans to modify their roaming and foraging ways and to congregate in

communities. In settle-
ments, they could rear
livestock, raise crops,
preserve fire, and pass down traditions.
Food is one of the clearest manifesta-
tions of the bounty of the Earth, and its
availability and variety are linked to the
rhythms of the land. Modern industrial-
ized and urban societies often take food
for granted; supermarkets are stuffed to
the brim, offering consumers a panoply
of foodstuffs no earlier civilization ever
imagined—and that only a few modern
nations enjoy. Hunger and malnourish-
ment inexorably surround the well-fed
societies as a reminder that poverty and
need are ever-present problems. That
some should feast while others starve has
always been among the cruelest ironies
of existence, a situation brought about
by both human greed and the vagaries of

nature. The abundance of
food in supermarkets
belies the fragile ecologi-
cal and economic balances of soil, weath-
er, technology, and geopolitics on which
the food supply depends. While limitless
bounty seems to be the whispered
promise of contemporary existence, a
broader examination of the condition of
the world indicates that the bounty is in
fact focused and restricted, and even
then capable of being upset by drought,
flood, pestilence, or human-generated
imbalances.

From the earliest times, food has
had powerful metaphorical usages in religious practice and definition. In the
Judeo-Christian tradition, food often
takes on spiritual significance. Adam and
Eve gave in to temptation when they ate
from the Tree of Knowledge; as a result

they were expelled from Paradise and forced to work the land for food. At the Last Supper, Jesus Christ transformed bread and wine into his body and blood, foretelling the sacrifice he would make for humankind.

The body and soul each require their mutual due, with needs that are not always exclusive. To eat, to be provided with the means to continue living, is a palpable metaphor of the largesse of God, and eating (or, in some cases, abstinence) often takes on a sacramental aura, as a celebration and recognition of divine bounty and care. In the Passover seder, the celebration of Ramadan, the Japanese tea ceremony, and in dietary laws of every faith, the gustatory rituals of life, dignified with traditional and spiritual overlays, are conscious and communal gestures toward a recognition of our place in the world.

It should come as no surprise that artists, as both participants in and visual chroniclers of their times, have regularly turned their attention to the many levels of meaning invested in the meal. Indeed, some of the earliest works of art known are images of animals that decorate the walls deep in the caves of southern Europe. Painted some twenty thousand years ago, long before the advent of writing, these images of reindeer, bison, and horses undoubtedly served some role in rituals of preparation for the hunt, as these animals would provide sustenance for the tribe. Beginning in antiquity, the Western tradition of art is replete with images of foodstuffs of every sort and variety. Wall paintings and mosaics from

ancient Egypt to Pompeii celebrate food. In tombs, they were often intended to provide nourishment in the afterlife; as decoration in homes, they served as an appealing reminder of temporal pleasures.

It was also in antiquity that the first images we can identify as real still lifes were created. Not all paintings that include food are still lifes, and not all still lifes involve food. But this genre has been a major—perhaps *the* major—vehicle for artistic ruminations on the edible world, and its traditions are inexorably linked to our culture's experience in depicting food. More than two thirds of the works highlighted in this book can be called pure still lifes. Strictly speaking, a still life is a depiction of dead or inert objects that have been arranged in a composition by an artist. An image of

oranges growing on a tree is not a still life, but a variant of landscape painting, as it portrays the fruits in their natural state. Those same oranges presented in a bowl on a table constitute a still life: the oranges are no longer alive, and their existence has been modified by the intervention of human activity and organization. Jean Baptiste Oudry's painting (plate 9) would satisfy most definitions of a still life but for the presence of the live monkey, whose activity presages a change in the painting's structure, diverting our attention from its still-life elements toward a consideration of narrative possibilities. Although the objects of a still life at times seem to be invested with energy and a potential for movement—as in the works of artists such as van Gogh and Braque (plate 20,

27), by definition, a still life exhibits objects at rest, presenting their elements for our considered and measured inspection, and implying that their condition will continue into the near future.

Still-life painting largely disappeared from Western art between the time of ancient Rome and the late sixteenth century. During this period, foodstuffs usually appeared as adjunct accoutrements in complex iconographic schemes, employed for their symbolic value within a strict religious construct. In Christian art of the time, an apple held by the Christ Child is not just a piece of fruit, but a reminder of the fall of Adam and Eve, and of the world's subsequent redemption through Christ and Mary. A pomegranate becomes a symbol of the Church, the fruit that holds a unity of many seeds. Grapes signify wine, and thus the blood of Christ; wheat stands for bread, which alludes to the body of Christ; salt reminds us of Lot's wife; and so on, until virtually all the food depicted in the art of this period seems part of a litany of faith. Leonardo da Vinci's *Last Supper*, perhaps the Renaissance's most celebrated painting of a meal, is located in a refectory adjacent to the monastic church of Santa Maria delle Grazie in Milan, in the room where members of the religious community shared their daily meals, visually reminded at every forkful of that other meal, so emblematic of Christ's sacrifice.

Toward the end of the sixteenth century, one of the most profound revolutions in the history of the visual arts occurred in a rather quiet manner. In response to a number of societal

changes—the Protestant Reformation, the rise of a more literate and inquisitive middle class, a change in the social status of artists, the incipient urges of what would eventually be called Humanism, and a shift in patronage toward a more structured capitalist system—new categories and formats of art began to appear throughout Europe. These included an intensification of interest in portraiture and the first consistent formulation of the parameters of landscape, genre, and still-life painting, all combining to begin to free imagery from its close links with specific religious practice. The spirit of invention and discovery that was transforming Europe and the world extended to the visual arts, and artists began to look more determinedly at the world around them.

This new pictorial independence did not mean, however, that the items analyzed by artists completely lost their metaphorical function. As attention shifted from a God-centered universe toward a human-centered world, the specific imagery artists employed also began to move from spiritual to allegorical and social realms. The development of new genres of painting in the seventeenth century increased the range of meanings associated with foods; now, rather than being restricted to religious symbolism, foods were related to the whole dizzying variety of human experience. A painting like Frans Snyders's monumental *Still Life with Dead Game, Fruits, and Vegetables in a Market* (plate 2) broadly exhibits the exuberance with which many artists embraced these changes. That a common Antwerp market stall would be lovingly described and

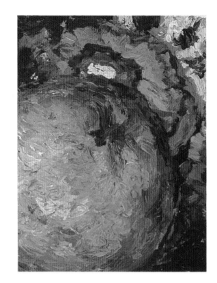

inspected on a scale until recently reserved for saints and heroes is a telling example of the changing perception of the function of art. Snyders's painting seeks to delight and inform, rather than to instruct and cajole, but it nonetheless retains a measure of a moral lesson. It is a democratic image, using the desire and requirement for food that every human understands to speak to a mass audience at an intuitive level. The mundane activities of humankind—in which, of course, food plays no small role—were no longer considered to be beneath observation; instead, they were sought out for their universal appeal. The untapped world of domestic life became new ground for artists to explore.

Attitudes toward food were a central part of this exploration of everyday experience. As still life began to take root as a new genre, its ability to accommodate a wide range of approaches became apparent. Food could speak to asceticism as well as to gluttony—the paucity of the poor person's repast could be rendered as well as the loaded tables of the rich. Rare or prized types of food were preserved and made visually secure in the painted image, which could be owned and enjoyed far longer than the perishable or exotic original. Scenes of every type of kitchen, banquet, market, hunt, and feast, with evocations of breakfast and dessert and all the culinary moments in between, glut the art of the seventeenth and eighteenth centuries, in which the inventory and subcategories of this pictorial approach were developed and refined. The table-top still life of a basket of fruit, illustrated here in a superb early example by Louise Moillon (plate 3),

became an especially popular vehicle for rendering food. Depicted in a plain and severe setting, Moillon's simple but perfectly described basket, filled with a variety of fruits and vegetables, indicates the comfort zone of middle-class life. To have food set casually about the house, presented as an indication of bounty as well as for decorative possibilities, bespeaks a fundamental security, an assurance of victory over hunger and want. The new middle class, from whom Moillon sprang and for whom this painting was intended, could look at food not as a scarce necessity, but as a luxury they commanded, a token of their own rising stature. Food could now stand for psychological and visual sustenance; it could delight and titillate in a language all audiences would recognize and understand.

The still life has been an inexhaustible source of delight for generation after generation of artists. From Chardin to Manet to van Gogh to Braque, it has provided a fount of pictorial intrigue, a perpetually malleable subject allowing for any number of subtle gradations of palette, texture, and composition. In the early history of still life, artists often used precise forms of realism to invest their subjects with a high degree of palpability; but by the eighteenth century, that tendency had begun to wane, and objects were frequently introduced and manipulated for their poetic and emotive possibilities. Even more than landscape painting or portraiture, still life is under the control of the artist: all its elements can be chosen, planned, adjusted, recast, and realigned. While always suggestive of gustatory,

tactile, and visual plea-sure, foods are, in essence, rather neutral subjects, carrying only stray hints of psychic baggage or reference. The still life provided artists with an opportunity for creative freedom of the widest sort, allowing them to invent a world that would respond to their every whim. Whether the painter's agenda was geared toward personal autobiography or stylistic investigation, food in a still-life setting proved to be a tremendously versatile subject, a playing field of surprisingly comprehensible equity.

In the past few decades many artists have begun to examine the mass psychology of food advertising and distribution. Soup cans painted by Andy Warhol do not actually depict food at all, but comment on a culture wherein the mechanics of presentation are more universally recognized and understood than the substances themselves. The idea of food begins yet again to extend to ideas of ownership and consumership, satiating areas of human desire other than simple hunger or thirst. Food, after all, will always be with us, and artists will always find ways for it to reflect and refract the human condition. It is the great equalizer, inscribed indelibly on our understanding of what it means to exist. Artists are certainly drawn to such stuff; after all, they have hungry eyes to feed as well.

SUGGESTED READING

Brettell, Richard. *French Impressionists*. Chicago: The Art Institute of Chicago, 1987.

Brettell, Richard. *French Salon Artists*, 1800–1900. Chicago: The Art Institute of Chicago, 1987.

Brettell, Richard. *Post-Impressionists*. Chicago: The Art Institute of Chicago, 1987.

Bryson, Norman. *Looking at the Overlooked: Four Essays on Still Life Painting*. Cambridge, Mass.: Harvard University Press, 1990.

Farb, Peter, and George Armelagos. *Consuming Passions: The Anthropology of Eating*. Boston: Houghton Mifflin, 1980.

Grieco, Allen J. *Themes in Art: The Meal*. London: Scala Publications Ltd, 1992.

Jordan, William B. *Spanish Still Life in the Golden Age: 1600–1650* (exhibition catalogue). Fort Worth: Kimbell Art Museum, 1985.

Mennell, Stephen. *All Manners of Food*. Oxford and New York: Basil Blackwell, 1985.

Schneider, Norbert. *The Art of the Still Life*. Cologne: Benedikt Taschen Verlag GmbH & Co., 1990.

Sterling, Charles. *Still-Life Painting from Antiquity to the Twentieth Century*. 2nd ed. New York: Harper & Row, 1981.

Tannahill, Reay. *Food in History*. New York: Stein and Day, 1973.

Trager, James. *The Foodbook*. New York: Grossman Publishers, 1970.

Weintraub, Linda (ed.). *Art What Thou Eat: Images of Food in American Art* (exhibition catalogue). Mount Kisco, NY: Moyer Bell Limited, 1991.

THE
PLATES

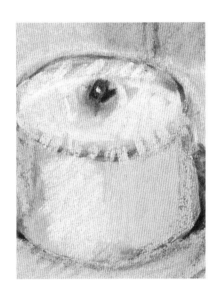

1

JUAN SANCHEZ COTAN

Spanish (1561-1627)
Still Life with Game Fowl, c. 1602
Oil on canvas; 26¹¹/₁₆ x 34¹⁵/₁₆ in.
Gift of Mr. and Mrs. Leigh B. Block, 1955.1203

Shortly after this painting was completed, Juan Sánchez Cotán left his home in Toledo and a twenty-year career devoted to still life to become a lay brother of the Carthusian Monastery of El Paular, where he dedicated himself to painting religious subjects. Scholars have sought, with justification, to read in his still lifes the incipient religious convictions that would lead him to alter his life so dramatically. Did Sánchez Cotán see the handiwork of God in every item in the world? Did he believe that the cabbage or the cucumber contains as much of the mystery of God's divine plan as does humankind? Did he believe, like his English contemporary William Shakespeare, that there is "a special Providence in the fall of a sparrow"? Why else would he have examined so closely and insistently in this and other compositions some rather humble foodstuffs set by a window? What drove this vision, what caused this fervent naturalism?

It is, in part, the great quality of this superb picture that provokes these and so many more questions. Sánchez Cotán arranged his elements like musical notes in some somnolent dirge. The ledge, lit sharply from the left, holds four items, while six more hang from an unseen support above, all in front of a dark, impenetrable void. Only the magnificent duck at the far right is allowed to overlap another item; all else is viewed singly, parallel to the picture plane, isolated for maximum visual analysis and delectation. Our eyes move around this painting in an unceasing circle; the strong curve set up by the bodies of the birds responds to a reverse arc in the array of fruits and vegetables. In this painting, Sánchez Cotán left us a perplexing and satisfying blend of specificity and mystery.

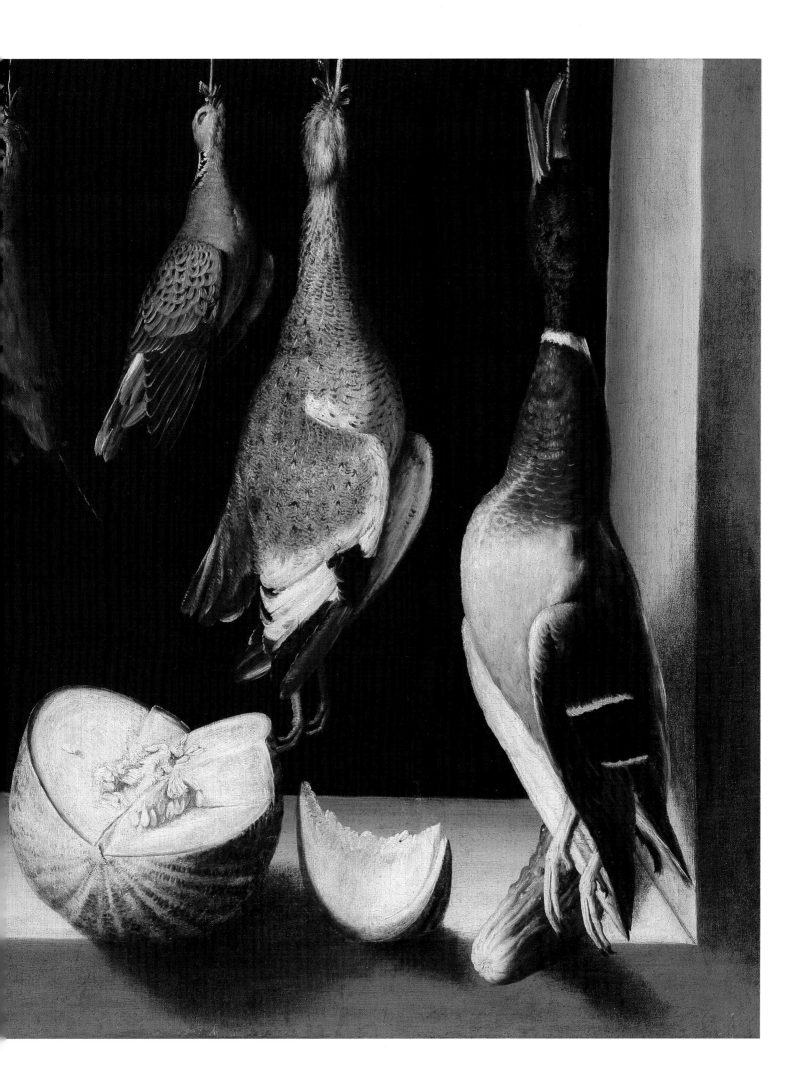

2

FRANS SNYDERS

Flemish (1579-1657)
*Still Life with Dead Game, Fruits, and
Vegetables in a Market,* 1614
Oil on canvas, 83 ¹/₂ x 121 ¹/₄ in.
Charles H. and Mary F. S. Worcester Fund
1981.182

In the seventeenth century, the first great age of pictorial specialization, few artists took on the new challenges in art more enthusiastically than Frans Snyders. While his colleagues throughout Northern Europe were beginning to carve their niches in categories like portraiture or landscape, in large paintings such as this Snyders boldly declared the parameters of his artistic turf. This work is a bravura testament to his powers as a painter of animals, or *animalier,* with some fine fruit still-life and genre painting thrown in for good measure. Here, Snyders used his consummate skills to render the incredible variety of foodstuffs humankind slaughters and larders for its table, making a painting that appears ready to burst, groaning under its own weight. Highly prized by collectors and connoisseurs both in Snyders's Flanders and abroad, imposing compositions such as this were placed in town houses or hunting lodges as entertaining and intriguing conversation pieces.

This exaggerated assemblage—there are more types of food here than could have been found at any one time at a single market stall in Snyders's Antwerp—features a dead swan poignantly spilling off the counter, set next to a hanging, gutted deer. Nearby, several brace of birds, a few dead rabbits, a peacock, and a boar's head (dripping blood, of course) round out the bounty. Attendant living animals are some pigeons, fighting roosters, and a peering cat, undoubtedly awaiting an opportunity to snatch a morsel. The ruler of this domain doffs his hat to the viewer while his pocket is picked by a ragamuffin. Snyders stuffed his composition with incident, filling the painting with drama from edge to edge. This all finally constitutes a vision of excess—an evocation of pictorial and dietary gluttony. The sense of surfeit that exudes from this picture is its own statement of success.

3

LOUISE MOILLON

French (1610-1696)
Still Life with a Basket of Fruit, 1630
Oil on panel; 21 x 28 ⅛ in.
Wirt D. Walker Fund (1948.78)

This painting is much more than just a superlative still life; it is also an important document in the history of the trials, tribulations, and, in this case, triumphs of female artists before the twentieth century. As a woman working in seventeenth-century France, Moillon was denied almost every means of access to a career in the visual arts. It would have been extremely difficult, not to mention outright illegal, for her to own a business, sign binding independent contracts, or negotiate payments. Her gender was denied most avenues of artistic training, and she was forbidden to study from the nude.

And, yet, Moillon is often cited as one of the key still-life painters of her time. She managed to overcome a sea of difficulties through a happy combination of circumstance and diligence. Moillon was the daughter and then the stepdaughter of men who were artists, and this undoubtedly enabled her to acquire the rudiments of artistic education. A document from 1620, when Moillon was still a child, certifies that profits from the sale of her works had to be shared with her stepfather. While she could not obtain the training to make her a painter of ancient, biblical, or modern history—the most revered thematic category in this epoch—she was able to use her eyes to look searchingly and persistently at the world around her. This painting, executed before Moillon was twenty years old, demonstrates the probity of her vision and her ability to use the painter's tools and materials to portray earthly substances. From peach to pea to plum to asparagus, Moillon achieved a powerful degree of verisimilitude, as she must have recognized when she signed her name with flourish at the bottom right of the composition.

4

Pieter Claesz
(Attributed to)

Dutch (1597/98-1661)
Still Life, c. 1630
Oil on panel; 18⅞ x 30¼ in.
Simeon B. Williams Fund (1935.300)

To the best of our knowledge, Pieter Claesz never painted anything except still lifes. He found all he needed as an artist in carefully composed arrangements of various items on a flat surface. These provided him with controlled universes, endlessly malleable and flexible, responsive to his every idea and desire. He spent a lifetime searching for the great satisfaction of a successful assemblage, of congregating his elements in just the right balance and degree to please both himself and his audience.

In this superb example of his craft, Claesz exhibited his great skills as a realist to astound us with his ability to make paint transubstantiate into his desired object, into lemon or platter, cookie or olive. But this painting is more than a display of pictorial skills; in it, Claesz made a formal examination of the possibilities and permutations of the oval. The rather low and oblique view he chose of this table makes oval sequences out of a roll, slices of lemons, a mince pie, the body of a pitcher, acorns, olives, plates, cookies, glasses, etc. This rendering of a dessert table is very carefully composed, and as full of visual delight as it is of the suggestion of gustatory pleasure. Cleverly placed diagonals—the knife at the bottom right, the spoon leading toward the pie—lead the eye into this amazing maze of stuff, all set crisply against a dark background that keeps our attention forever reverberating around this loaded spread. A white tablecloth covers three-quarters of the table, its crisp folds creating vertical pillars that further animate the composition. The lace filigree at its end smooths its juxtaposition with the rose-colored undercloth. The mince pie, the literal center and heart of this painting, is the crowning moment in this paean of dessert. Its bounty spills out of the crust in rampant munificence; note how Claesz showed us the differing fates of a cooked fruit slice in the pie from the fresh lemon slices just below it.

PETER PAUL RUBENS

Flemish (1577-1640)
Wedding of Peleus and Thetis, 1636
Oil on panel, 10 ³/₄ x 16 ⁷/₈ in.
Charles H. and Mary F. S. Worcester Collection,
1947.108

This is the wedding feast that led to the Trojan War. Peleus, King of the Myrmidons, and the Goddess Thetis—shown at the painting's right—enjoy their nuptial supper surrounded by Greek gods. The daughter of Zeus and Hera, Eris, whose name aptly means "discord," was not invited. Her anger at this slight led her to a cruel revenge; before flying away, as seen at the top, she threw a golden apple marked "for the fairest" onto the wedding table. Zeus, at center, picks it up, and the trouble begins. His wife, Hera, reaches for the apple, as does the armor-clad Athena from across the table, while voluptuous Aphrodite points to herself as the obvious recipient of the prize. Zeus, unwilling to make the choice, subsequently named the Trojan hero Paris to select the winner; this led to intense politicking among the goddesses, with Aphrodite promising Paris the most beautiful woman in the world, Helen of Mycenae, if he chose her. He did and received the love of Helen, followed by the anger of her husband, Agamemnon, ten years of war, and the eventual destruction of Troy by the Greeks.

Rubens painted this lively and rhythmic oil as a sketch for a cycle of over sixty paintings on the loves of the gods for the hunting lodge of King Philip IV of Spain. Rubens's awesome skills extended to politics. Sent on a diplomatic mission to Spain in 1628, he so impressed the monarch that he received many royal commissions. This immense cycle could not be painted by one person alone; Rubens made sketches such as this as models for his assistants and collaborators. (In this case, Jacob Jordaens did the final, much larger, picture.) The ambitious dimensions of this commission reflect the extensive imperial power of the monarchy in the seventeenth century and the international prominence of Flanders's greatest Baroque painter.

PAOLO ANTONIO BARBIERI
(ATTRIBUTED TO)

Italian (1603-1649)
Kitchen Still Life, c. 1640
Oil on canvas; 26 ⅛ x 31 ³/₁₆ in.
A. A. Munger Collection (1934.389)

Paolo Antonio Barbieri was the younger brother of Giovanni Francesco Barbieri, who was one of the greatest Italian Baroque painters, much better known by his nickname, Guercino (meaning squint-eyed). Paolo's genealogically subservient status may have limited his artistic ambition; he spent his entire life in the service of his brother, often as an anonymous assistant. While Guercino was the honored painter to popes and kings, Paolo remained in the background, very much the junior partner in the family business. In 1629, he began keeping an account book—the *Libro dei Conti*—wherein he catalogued his brother's massive artistic output and added to its pages a listing of his own modest oeuvre, comprised totally of still-life and genre paintings.

The *Libro dei Conti* mentions Paolo's many compositions of fruit, fish, flowers, spice goods, and silverware, etc., along with the quite small sums these pictures fetched. This meditative painting depicts mushrooms, grapes, almonds, chestnuts, and two ripe cheeses on a napkin, all sitting on a spare kitchen shelf. There is a prosaic rhythm to this sequence of circular and oval forms; a raking light extending from the right forcefully suggests their volume. Each object is rendered with meticulous care, and the colors are measured and balanced. This is a sober and satisfying effort, and a terse essay in the process of observation.

7

JUAN DE ZURBARAN
(ATTRIBUTED TO)

Spanish (1620-1649)
Flowers and Fruit in a China Bowl, c. 1645
Oil on canvas; 32½ x 42¾ in.
Wirt D. Walker Fund (1947.511)

A fine example of seventeenth-century Spanish still life, this painting is notable for its focused and ascetic quality, intense concentration on the palpability of substances, consummate treatment of light/dark relationships, and insistent and skilled use of optical realism. Its connection to the traditions exemplified in Spanish art by artists such as Juan Sánchez Cotán (see plate 1) is readily apparent. Recently, scholars have convincingly attributed this painting to Juan de Zurbarán, who was the son of the renowned painter Francisco de Zurbarán. Juan's brief career—he died of the bubonic plague in Seville at the age of twenty-nine—makes a considered understanding of the range of his aesthetic rather difficult. Only three paintings signed by him exist today; all are still lifes that bear a close relationship to this painting.

The pears that fill this delicate ceramic bowl to its brim seem to radiate with the searing heat of Spain. Their skins are almost blistered with sunburn, and setting them against the cool ivory whiteness of the bowl emphasizes their warmth. The golden surfaces of the pears almost seem to be the source of light in this composition; the quinces and flowers that loosely encircle them appear to receive light from the more tightly organized fruits displayed at the center. The beautifully and patiently rendered vertical fluting of the ceramic bowl imposes structure amidst the more chaotic silhouettes of fruits and flowers. The painting is an essay in discipline that delights in a summoning of apparent opposites: light and dark, warm and cool, order and chance. It everywhere manages to convey the life that can surge beneath austere surfaces, and to illustrate once again the unexpected drama that can reside within something as simple as a bowl of fruit and flowers.

8

GIUSEPPE MARIA CRESPI

Italian (1665-1747)
The Marriage at Cana, c. 1686
Oil on canvas; 74 x 97¾ in.
Wirt D. Walker Fund (1956.129)

This large painting by Crespi is one of the later masterworks of the grand Italian tradition of sumptuous feast paintings. Especially in Venetian painting, as in the works of Bassano, Titian, Tintoretto, and Veronese, a public miracle in the life of Christ occasioned rich immersion into the visual pleasures of the world, mixing the secular and religious spheres in a broad and vibrantly theatrical composition. The delights and possibilities of this format reached at least as far as Crespi's Bologna, and this painting is one of his earliest major efforts.

Accompanied by his mother, Jesus attended a wedding in Cana (John 2:1-10). When the wine ran out, he asked that six vessels be filled with water, which he then miraculously turned into wine. Jesus sits at the table next to Mary at the far left of this composition, his profile function-ing almost like a fulcrum setting into motion a long diagonal that travels through the large stringed instrument played by the musician, end-ing with the golden vessel at the lower right. An even more powerful diagonal is set up by the angle of the nuptial table. The bride's father, seated between his daughter and Mary, seems to ask Jesus to explain the miraculous event that has just occurred. Jesus appears to acknowledge responsibility, pointing to an empty flask at his feet, next to which lies an ennervated canine. In contrast, at the lower right of the painting is a presumably full jug, whose upright position is threatened by a mischievous feline. The rest of the company stirs tentatively and nervously as they begin to realize what has happened. The high level of activity in the kitchen at the upper left, the display of fine silver and gold dinnerware at the right and on the linen-covered table, and the number of servants involved in the event undoubtedly reflects the splendor of special feasts enjoyed by wealthy Italians in the late sev-enteenth century, as opposed to the modest wed-ding attended by Jesus and Mary.

9

JEAN BAPTISTE OUDRY

French (1686-1755)
Still Life with Monkey, Fruits, and Flowers, 1724
Oil on canvas; 56 x 57 ¹/₁₆ in.
Major Acquisitions Centennial Fund (1977.486)

While Chardin (see plate 10) might now be recognized as eighteenth-century France's greatest still-life painter, he was not without competition during his lifetime. Many patrons found Chardin's compositions too somber and ordinary, lacking uplifting qualities of elegance and charm. Royal patrons such as Louis XV and the king of Denmark, for example, turned to the older Jean Baptiste Oudry for still-life painting that was lighter in color and mood, filled with amusing details and graceful accomplishments. Oudry brought to still life some of the thrill of the outdoors and the hunt, often utilizing game and landscape elements in his compositions.

The frivolous and sparkling aura of the Rococo court of Versailles saturates this painting. The impish pet monkey, loose among the gardens, picks some grapes from a well-stocked little hamper, his thieving nature more seductive than threatening. Unlike modern times, when fresh produce is available year-round, fruits such as these were a luxury enjoyed only a few months each year. Oudry's fruits are ready to burst with their own fullness, his flowers to explode in ethereal glory. Delicately colored, exquisitely composed pictures such as this decorated the salons of an aristocratic elite, expressing a privileged way of life that would be harshly amended by the revolutions to come.

10

JEAN BAPTISTE SIMEON CHARDIN

French (1699-1779)
The White Tablecloth, c. 1730/32
Oil on canvas; 38 x 48⁵⁄₁₆ in.
Mr. and Mrs. Lewis Larned Coburn Memorial
Collection (1944.699)

The impact Chardin had on the history of still-life painting cannot be overexaggerated. When his career began, the genre was considered by the prestigious French Academy to be the lowest kind of artmaking, beneath religious and history painting, portraiture, landscape, and scenes of everyday life. The still life, it was thought, required only an act of mimicry, comprised of the simple and unintellectual task of rendering inanimate objects in plain settings. By the end of his life, Chardin had become a senior officer of that very Academy, and an artist whose work was highly prized by art collectors throughout Europe. He did not rehabilitate still-life painting as much as he plumbed its essences, making it eloquent and substantial and finding in its modesty glimpses of transcendental truth. Chardin's great gift is that he never required trumpets and fanfare to capture a viewer's attention: He could do so with just a few simple objects, whose formal beauty and dignity he understood and communicated.

Little could be more modest or down to earth than this plain, round table, adorned by nothing more than a carelessly placed white tablecloth, a crusty loaf of bread, two glasses, a knife, and some sausage on a tray, all set next to a quite pedestrian bucket. This simple context for a repast is simply presented, straightforward, and unassuming. And yet it is profoundly evocative, a rendering of what is taken for granted, seeable but unexamined, a measured and purposeful slowing of tempo calling for reflection and consideration. While spare, the painting seems full; each object appears to have found its inevitable place within the composition. Chardin revealed poetry and humanity in all his subjects; and his patient, loving examination imbues them with stature and weight. This is a table of nourishment in every sense of the word.

11

RAPHAELLE PEALE

American (1774-1825)
Strawberries, Nuts, etc., 1822
Oil on panel; 16 3/8 x 22 3/4 in.
Gift of Jamee J. and Marshall Field (1991.100)

It is probably overly romantic to think that some people were predestined to become artists, born to their craft with inherited skills and inclinations. The case of Raphaelle Peale, however, provides some evidence for that notion. He was the first of Charles Willson Peale's seventeen offspring to survive into adulthood; like many of his siblings (Rembrandt, Vandyke, Rubens, MichaelAngelo, Titian, Angelica, Sophonisba, and Rosalba), he was named for one of his father's many favorite artists. Peale was one of Revolutionary America's great characters—an artist, inventor, naturalist, museum proprietor, and writer, and the good friend of George Washington and Benjamin Franklin. He trained his son Raphaelle well; by the age of twelve, he was working by his father's side, and, by seventeen, he was doing independent portraits.

It was to still life, though, that Raphaelle Peale gravitated. He exhibited eight still lifes at Philadelphia's Columbianum exhibition in 1795, and concentrated on this genre for the rest of his somewhat troubled career. The long shadow of his distinguished father, a painful and progressive case of gout, and heavy drinking largely restricted Raphaelle to still life. But, within that area, his accomplishment is profound; Peale had an innate sensitivity for the poetry of objects, and for how they could be arranged into almost classical compositions. Each thing is seen and described singly and with unerring accuracy, but also ineluctably works in concert with its neighbor and with the entire composition. Color, shape, and substance are carefully weighed and organized. Here, a plain setting is bejeweled with an evocation of dessert, one of rare and highly desirable fruit and nuts, as well as with Chinese export pottery, which was highly coveted at the time. The compote jar of strawberries is particularly fine in its rendering, permitting the artist to exhibit his skill in depicting the berries through glass.

Raphaelle Peale Pinxt 1822

12

EDOUARD MANET

French (1832-1883)
Still Life with Carp, 1864
Oil on canvas; 28⅞ x 36¼ in.
Mr. and Mrs. Lewis Larned Coburn Memorial
Collection (1942.311)

In 1864, when Manet painted this picture, he was already among the most controversial artists in France. In the Salon of 1864, and in the year before, at the Salon des Refusés, his work had been singled out for critical excoriation. Manet's art had come to symbolize, for conservatives and radicals alike, the overturning of cherished values and the fevered quest for the new; paintings such as *Still Life with Carp* were considered almost revolutionary, ill-mannered assaults on tradition and public taste.

This response was, in fact, not what Manet expected or desired. He was attracted to the precedents of many Old Master traditions, making overt references in his compositions to the work of Baroque and Rococo artists he admired. In this canvas, he paid homage to the bold materiality of seventeenth-century Dutch and Flemish still lifes (see plate 2), and to the sophisticated simplicity of the art of Chardin (see plate 10).

Nonetheless, it is not hard to understand why Manet's art proved to be so unsettling for the French public. Still-life painting had been regarded, after all, as a relatively well-behaved genre. It was usually restful, filled with precise observation, and dedicated to depicting delightful combinations of fruit and/or flowers. In *Still Life with Carp* and other works, Manet challenged this placid tradition by dispensing with its niceties and by subjecting his viewers to pungent slices of life in the raw. These fish are to be eaten, not to be admired for their aesthetic grace or for the poetry of their placement. Manet's choice of a close view and his use of a palette knife and bold brushwork add to the composition's confrontative quality. In this still life, Manet searched for and found power instead of grace. His unapologetic directness breathed new life into this format.

13

IGNACE HENRI JEAN THEODORE FANTIN-LATOUR

French (1836-1904)
Still Life: Corner of a Table, 1873
Oil on canvas; 37^{15}/$_{16}$ x 49^{3}/$_{16}$ in.
Ada Turnball Hertle Fund (1951.226)

This painting has a casual and leisurely air to it, the kind of seemingly accidental composition that is actually the result of great artistic skill and understanding. It can be seen as one of the finest portraits of nineteenth-century life in Paris, without the physical presence of a single human being. People are undoubtedly grouped just off to the right or left, arguing about Richard Wagner's latest opera; gossiping about some actress; discussing the radical recent work of Degas, Manet, and Monet; or exclaiming over the open sexuality in Zola's new novel.

The elegant portraitist and still-life painter Fantin-Latour suggested here the scintillating life of a great capital at the height of its powers by showing just a section of a table visited for pleasure and then left behind. Objects are strewn across it with a randomness indicating the effortless indolence of a very wealthy and comfortable culture. Wine and food are here luxurious diversions to please a refined palate. In selecting the low viewpoint and in truncating the rhododendron plant, Fantin-Latour utilized the compositional strategy of cropping that had recently been introduced to France through Japanese prints and photography. The artist's virtuoso brushwork calls his objects into focus without a trace of effort or strain. At this table of manners, elegant people congregated for visual as well as gustatory sustenance.

14

ADOLPHE JOSEPH MONTICELLI

French (1824-1886)
Still Life with Fruit and Wine Jug, 1874
Oil on canvas; 19 x 23½ in.
Gift of Mary and Leigh Block (1988.261)

By the time he did this painting, Monticelli had returned to his native Marseilles after spending some fifteen years in Paris. There, he had witnessed, and participated in, one of the great art controversies of his time. Should paint be applied with gusto, slathered on the surface of a canvas with force and panache, always calling attention to its own materiality, or should it be subjugated to the objects that it describes, applied with restraint and delicacy, emphasizing the subject more than the painter? This dichotomy, which was perceived as a conflict between the uses of color and line, preoccupied many artists and critics, and there is little doubt where Monticelli's heart lay.

Known as painterly paintings, Monticelli's canvases are virtually encrusted with thickly applied pigment. Even richness of color was less important to the artist than was its substance as paint: Note how limited in tone this painting is, and how restrained in chroma. The liquidity of oil pigment was as constant and crucial an assertion to Monticelli as the pear or glass it might describe; he saw little conflict in this and, in Marseilles, he extended the dialogue between the eye and the object to include the hand and the brush. Few artists in the nineteenth century were more painterly than Monticelli. Influenced by Titian, Rembrandt, and Delacroix, among others, he was to influence, in turn, younger artists such as Cézanne (see plate 17) and van Gogh (see plate 20).

15

FRANÇOIS SAINT BONVIN

French (1817-1887)
The Maid, c. 1875
Oil on canvas; 18 3/8 x 12 7/8 in.
Mr. and Mrs. Martin A. Ryerson Collection
(1933.1110)

Nineteenth-century French artists felt so secure in the position of their country as a center of world culture and learning that they began systematically to examine their own art history, seeking in the past the harbingers of its present glory. Bonvin was a largely self-taught artist who started to work seriously as a painter while he was employed as a clerk by the police department in Paris. Fascinated with still-life painting and with scenes of everyday life, he became one of the steadily growing group of amateurs and connoisseurs that scoured France for paintings on these themes by long-dead artists such as Chardin (see plate 10), artists who had been almost completely forgotten but who were being resurrected and re-examined as exemplars of earlier French achievement.

This painting is clearly an homage to Chardin, with a nod as well to the "Little Masters" of seventeenth-century Holland. The maid at work in the kitchen, her honest labor the underpinning of the home, was a favorite theme often utilized by Chardin and his Dutch predecessors. But that does not make this a conservative or backward-looking image. To employ historical nostalgia to show one's cognizance of this tradition in art was actually quite a modern thing to do, since it also celebrated rural life, which was being threatened and marginalized by the Industrial Revolution and the resulting growth of large cities. By the time Bonvin painted this picture, he had moved away in some disgust from Paris to settle in the small village of St. Germain-en-Laye, where he would stay until his death. As city dwellers began

to romanticize rural life as symbolic of clean air, good health, slower pace, and timeless moral values that modern urban life, fast-changing and degraded as it was, could not provide, it is not surprising that faintly anecdotal paintings of such subjects were in high demand, and several paintings by Bonvin were purchased by the Louvre while he was still alive. As one liberal critic, Pierre Petroz, wrote of the art of Bonvin's contemporary, the more famous Jean François Millet: "He knows how to give the simplest rural work a biblical grandeur. . . . His figures do not pose; they work with ardor and in such a way as to make us regard human labor with veneration."

The spirituality that Millet and Bonvin saw manifest so powerfully in rural labor is very clearly present here. With the ritualistic dignity of someone performing a timeless sacrament, the maid pours blood from a flayed ox's head that she will prepare into the French delicacy known as headcheese. It seems to be a very neat operation; if her pristine costume is stained, we cannot tell, since her posture delicately shields us from most of the gory aspects of her activity. In fact, were it not for the eye hole and stream of blood pouring into the white bowl, we might think she is cutting a large loaf of peasant bread. Bonvin's carefully orchestrated color scheme, with notes of intense color—the maid's close-fitting white cap, brilliant red blouse, and boldly striped skirt—against a dark background, and the inclusion of only minimal detail, such as the leek that has fallen on the floor, add to the focus and gravity of the scene.

16

PIERRE AUGUSTE RENOIR

French (1841-1919)
The Rowers' Lunch, 1875-76
Oil on canvas; 21^{11}/$_{16}$ x 25^{15}/$_{16}$ in.
Potter Palmer Collection (1922.437)

Artists, writers, and social and cultural historians alike have emphasized the dispiriting and tawdry aspects of the Industrial Revolution. We are all familiar with how it encouraged child labor, pollution, urban slums, and endless social exploitation. Though they cannot refute these assertions, the paintings of Pierre Auguste Renoir and other Impressionists, while delivering a skewed and prettified version of their time, do present another side of the story.

One of humankind's great adventures, the Industrial Revolution should also be credited for an expansion in leisure time and disposable income; and for the rise of a more prosperous and better-educated middle class. In this painting, a few of this group are casually seated around a table, enjoying a holiday from the city, chatting, smoking, and imbibing, all while being caressed by the warm air of a glorious summer day in the environs of Paris. Their labors elsewhere may be heavy, but their rest here is delightful, a hard-won indolence earned by the sweat of their brows. The painting exudes a state of relaxation rarely equaled in the history of art, due to Renoir's light, almost evanescent touch. His loose brushwork and the activity he described here seem linked, in concert, without strain or dissonance. This permits us to meander aimlessly around the picture, vicariously enjoying the fruits of the fruits of labor.

17

PAUL CEZANNE

French (1839-1906)
The Plate of Apples, c. 1877
Oil on canvas; 18 x 21½ in.
Gift of Kate L. Brewster (1949.512)

There is a wonderful moment in Woody Allen's film *Manhattan* when he cites his list of the things he believes are good reasons for continuing to live. Among them, he includes "Cézanne's apples." That fruit, as painted over and over by that painter, has come to symbolize the victory that can follow the struggle of an artist to achieve his or her vision. If nothing else, then, this painting provides us with some twenty more reasons for living.

Fruit has long been regarded as a gift of God that humankind earns after long and hard labor. Understood in this light, Cézanne's constant choice of apples as a subject is particularly apt. In each of his studies of the fruit, Cézanne did battle after battle with sphere after sphere, trying to realize what he called his "little sensations," attempting to reconcile his hand to his eye and the experience of the moment with the expression of long-standing, much-revered principles of art. Even when huddled together as they are here, Cézanne's apples are really separate and distinct episodes of his effort to give them weight and substance. Each is its own arena, a permanent record of his ongoing engagement with his skills and search for successful pictorial articulation. That search extends to his bold treatment of the tablecloth and edges, and to his incessant fussing with the pattern of the wallpaper, always adjusting, reworking, and recalibrating.

Cézanne spent most of his life in the south of France, and managed to keep a certain distance from the Parisian art world. His relative solitude provided the laboratory his aesthetic required, the context for complete concentration and single-minded focus. Cézanne's still-life paintings are nothing if not honest, exhibiting in every hard-won stroke the dignity and worth of the artist's efforts.

18

CLAUDE MONET

French (1840-1926)
Still Life: Apples and Grapes, 1880
Oil on canvas; 26¹/₁₆ x 32³/₈ in.
Mr. and Mrs. Martin A. Ryerson Collection
(1933.1152)

Only between 1878 and 1882 did Monet concentrate on still-life painting with any regularity; throughout his career, he was preoccupied with exploring the possibilities of landscape painting—the varied magnificence of country and city, and the myriad effects of sunlight and vision. (There's an old—and untrue—story that only when it rained day after day would Monet, bored and unable to encounter nature, consent to paint still lifes.) The scope of the world existing on a table-top may have seemed restrictive to an eye inspired by the glories of the grand outdoors, but Monet's still lifes are beautiful statements of his vision. His stupendous skills as a colorist and his shimmering brushwork clearly pulse through these apples and grapes; the low viewpoint of this table also turns this painting into a landscape of still-life elements, with apples and grapes standing in for bushes and haystacks.

Cooking apples are at the left, their broad and beefy massiveness a foil for the smaller eating apples at the right. Different types of grapes cascade from a small basket. Monet enriched this basic set-up with a rainbow of color; the painting exudes chromatic splendor, with pinks, lavenders, purples, vermillions, light greens, and blues. His brush orchestrated his optical experiences, translating what his eyes encountered into another type of experience, one everywhere reflecting and refracting the activities of seeing and painting.

19

PIERRE AUGUSTE RENOIR

French (1841-1919)
Fruits from the Midi, 1881
Oil on canvas; 19 15/16 x 25 11/16 in.
Mr. and Mrs. Martin A. Ryerson Collection
(1933.1176)

In 1881, Renoir began two years of almost incessant travel. He visited Algiers twice, as well as Venice, Rome, Florence, Naples, and Palermo (where he did a portrait of the composer Richard Wagner); he spent some time with Cézanne in L'Estaque; and he made many stops across the Midi (the south of France). This marked Renoir's first extensive exposure to this part of the world, and, not surprisingly, his paintings of this period reflect his heightened interest in things southern and his firsthand experience of the bright and penetrating light of the Mediterranean world.

In *Fruits from the Midi,* Renoir replaced the apples, pears, and grapes of the North with more southern produce: eggplants, tomatoes, red peppers, tangerines, pomegranates, and lemons. These fruits (technically, they can all be called fruits) required sharp and pungent colors, ranging from the deep black-purples of the eggplants to the hot oranges of the peppers and the acid yellows of the lemons. Renoir's painting has a high temperature and pitch; its rather haphazard composition, the succulence of the produce, and the painting's intense warmth all signal a relaxation of the formal rigidities of the still-life tradition that is ultimately very seductive.

20

VINCENT VAN GOGH

Dutch (1853-1890)
Still Life: Fruit, c. 1887
Oil on canvas; 18¼ x 21¾ in.
Gift of Kate L. Brewster (1949.215)

These are fruits on fire, vehicles for a passion almost too intense to be circumscribed with oil paint. Van Gogh's curiously spaceless arrangement of fruits—just what are they lying on?—seems to pulsate with what, to modern eyes, resembles radioactivity, as if their life-force can be seen emanating around them. We can imagine van Gogh's hand darting restlessly around his elements, building up their surfaces with slashing and flickering brush strokes loaded with paint. There is certainly nothing still about this still life; instead, there is everywhere a throbbing of energy, a relentless and almost exhausting rhythm.

An old truism holds that every work of art is a self-portrait of its maker. Take, for example, the still lifes in these pages by Cézanne, Monet, Renoir, and van Gogh. All four were made within a single decade in the same country, and all are composed of roughly the same elements presented in similar contexts. And yet how extraordinarily different they are! It is not apples or grapes that finally distinguish them from one another; rather, it is their handling and interpretation, the personal agendas that are somehow inexorably woven throughout the ambitions and strategies played out in table-top and fruit. Van Gogh's rapid assault on these bits of fruit expresses not only the intensity of his personality but also artistic impetuosity and virtuosity of the highest order.

21

James Ensor

Belgian (1860-1949)
Still Life with Fish and Shells, 1888
Oil on canvas; 31⅞ x 39½ in.
Gift of Mary and Leigh Block (1978.96)

Ostend is best known today as a port for ferries
running between England and the Continent.
Millions pass through the Belgian seaside resort
town every year; like Dover or Calais, it has
become a place of transit, a stop on the way to
somewhere else. Ensor lived in Ostend for most
of his life. His parents ran a souvenir shop there,
selling such things as seashells, crockery, toys,
and local bric-a-brac. This pinkish still life suggests a variation of a shelf in a shop like that of
Ensor's parents, where the wares of Ostend were
presented for the delectation of the passing
tourist.

In Ostend, Ensor developed one of the most
isolated and unique visions of his time. His paintings can be overt and powerful assaults on the
senses, satirical fantasies of an insane world, or
subtle and mysterious evocations of scenarios
where things are just a bit askew. Well aware of
his Flemish roots, in pictures such as this, Ensor
consciously evoked the tradition of naturalistic
still life painting as practiced by Snyders (see
plate 2). And yet, there is a world of difference
between them. This composition, including a
variety of fruits of the sea arranged among bas-
kets and ceramic vessels, is somehow tense and
dry, tinged with a scratchy weirdness. A puzzling
presentation piece, it leaves us unsure and ques-
tioning. Perhaps its strident, odd character is due
to the power of childhood memories its subject
invoked in Ensor. Remembering his parents'
inventory, which was stored in the family's attic,
he stated: "I was . . . fascinated by our dark and
frightening attic, full of horrible spiders,
seashells, plants and animals from distant seas,
beautiful chinaware, rust and blood-colored
effects, red and white coral, monkeys, turtles,
dried mermaids and stuffed Chinamen."

22

William Glackens

American (1870-1938)
At Mouquin's, 1905
Oil on canvas; 48³/₁₆ x 36¹/₄ in.
Friends of American Art Collection (1925.295)

By the beginning of the twentieth century, New York had confirmed its status as the United States' most cosmopolitan city with a growing number of restaurants based on chic and upscale European models. Located on Sixth Avenue in New York, just two blocks from Glackens's studio, Mouquin's restaurant provided a vibrant and convivial meeting place for fashionable New Yorkers, drawn from both inside and outside the art world. There, they would see and be seen, eat and drink, and gossip and argue about the issues of the day. The second-floor dining room and first-floor café, pictured here, impressed with their sophisticated, Continental cuisine. While the striking woman shown here cannot be identified, her companion is the painter's good friend, the lawyer and bon vivant James Moore, who actually owned a rival restaurant nearby. The serpentine (and anatomically suspect—it is difficult to reconcile the placement of her shoulders and hips) curve running through the woman's brilliant blue gown is lovingly and vivaciously depicted by the artist. In the mirror behind them can be seen Glackens's wife and another friend. The dynamic brushwork, the off-center composition, the couple's assertive presence, and, in particular, Moore's beefy face and forthright manner, exude the energy of the era of then-President Teddy Roosevelt, reflecting a nation coming of age, ready to assert itself as a center of culture and good living.

Everywhere in Glackens's picture, however, that assertion is still largely couched in the French language. His sparkling style is based on his study of French art, particularly that of Manet and the Impressionists. The placement of figures against a mirror and the broadly and beautifully painted still life of bottles and of flowers in a glass are strongly reminiscent of Manet's *Bar at the Folies-Bergère* (London,

Courtauld Institute), in the same way that the glistening interior of Mouquin's itself appears to have imitated Parisian café prototypes. Even the somewhat remote expression of the figures recalls the aloofness of the clientele of the bars and eateries of Paris as depicted in paintings by Henri de Toulouse-Lautrec and others. America was not yet fully verbal in its own distinct voice (for much of its history, this painting was known as "Chez Mouquin's"), but was still eager to show its sophistication through the imitation of supposedly superior European cultural examples. But Glackens's canvas does not just reflect the absorption of visual models—following a pattern of behavior assumed by denizens of Europe's largest cities in response to the difficulties of living in too close proximity to others, New Yorkers, as this picture seems to confirm, had developed a stance of protective distance from one another as well.

Obviously proud of this painting, Glackens included it in the first exhibition, held at the MacBeth Gallery in New York in 1908, of a group of artists which strongly disapproving critics dubbed the Ash Can School because of its devotion to making straightforward images of modern American life. While this painting seems nothing but lovely to modern eyes, many in Glackens's own time thought otherwise. One particularly incensed writer exclaimed: "Vulgarity smites one in the face at this exhibition, and I defy you to find anyone in a healthy frame of mind who for instance wants to hang . . . Glackens' 'At Mouquin's' . . . in his living room or gallery and not get disgusted two days later. Is it fine art to exhibit our sores?" The writer was probably objecting to the composition's exhibition of what he felt were the loose morals of the day, rather than to deficiencies in the painting itself.

23

JOHN SLOAN

American (1871-1951)
Renganeschi's, Saturday Night, 1912
Oil on canvas; 26⁵/₁₆ x 32¹/₈ in.
Gift of Mary Otis Jenkins (1926.1580)

Like Glackens (see plate 22) a charter member of the Ash Can School, Sloan focused much of his painting, as well as his magazine and newspaper illustration, on the ramifications of modern urban life. One of the anecdotes told about Sloan concerns his indefatigable wanderings around New York. Consumed by the texture of the bustling city, he would roam the streets for hours, foraging for visual incidents he might later incorporate into his art. Even in his studio, he remained a voracious observer: Some of his paintings were inspired by the views of tenement roofs afforded by the studio's window, as he watched the lives of his neighbors.

While a Socialist from 1910 on, Sloan was no doctrinaire, never a propagandist for any specific political agenda. His art is fired with a zest for life, for capturing all the habits and vagaries of an urban populace. As he noted in his journal on April 15, 1909, "I am rather more interested in the human beings themselves than in schemes for betterment." This seemingly haphazard composition emphasizes the intense atmosphere of this busy, noisy restaurant, which was located on 10th Street in Greenwich Village. The convivial crowd contains many young women, leading more independent lives than their mothers had. It is easy to sense Sloan there too, watching and sketching, the voyeur consumed by his interest in the activities of others. His unquenchable curiosity about and sympathy with his subjects earns him the appellation of humanist.

24

MARSDEN HARTLEY

American (1877-1943)
Movement No. 10, 1917
Oil on construction board; 15 ¼ x 19 ½ in.
Alfred Stieglitz Collection (1949.548)

This painting, whose title probably refers to music, as in one section of a composition, actually reflects a very tense moment in Hartley's life. Before World War I, Hartley had been on his way to enjoying a vibrant career at the vanguard of modern art. The great photographer and leader of the New York avant-garde, Alfred Stieglitz, who once owned this painting, had introduced Hartley to the art of Cézanne and Picasso and had shown the young artist's work at his gallery, 291, as early as 1909. Hartley made several trips to Europe, moved in Gertrude Stein's Parisian circle, and, in 1912, met and discussed his art with the Russian abstract painter Wassily Kandinsky, who often thought of his paintings as analogous to music and entitled them accordingly. At that time, Hartley became a passionate Germanophile; he admired the pomp and ceremony of imperial Germany and commenced an intense love relationship with a young lieutenant, Karl von Freyburg. Hartley's work between 1912 and 1914 is among his finest and most joyous, fusing images of German military flags and insignia with high-keyed, decorative impulses to create the most advanced, abstract art by any American at that time.

But then came the war. Von Freyburg was killed in 1914. The last American painter of note to leave Europe, Hartley found that, upon his forced return to the United States, German imagery and sympathies were unpalatable to his previously enthusiastic audience. During the remaining war years, his art reflects a need for order, a search for healing and, perhaps, for forgetfulness, which he satisfied by focusing solely on his craft. The subdued tones and dignified composition of this painting are stark indeed, suggesting degrees of mourning and calm resolve. The simple rhythms and stoic probity of this plate of fruit seem a call for maturation and peace, a confirmation of simple pleasures, and a withdrawal from a world gone mad.

25

CHARLES DEMUTH

American (1883-1935)
Eggplant and Plums, 1922-23
Watercolor over graphite on paper;
11⁷⁄₈ x 18¹⁄₈ in.
Olivia Shaler Swan Memorial Collection (1933.470)

In this spry and vibrant watercolor, Demuth seems to have engaged himself with the color purple in order to explore color value and saturation. He willed everything else away; the broad expanse of untouched, or barely touched, white paper makes a striking backdrop for these majestic fruit forms. Demuth recorded the warmer, more winelike purples of the eggplants against the cooler, deeper blues of the plums; the swollen bodies of both fruits are sensitively and economically evoked with a minimum of effort to suggest their setting and a maximum amount of attention to capturing their particular visual natures. Even the gray-purple shadows cast by these fruits are considered and weighed. A superb watercolorist, Demuth exploited the medium's possibilities with great effect; his brush both delicately and restlessly washed his surface, suggesting just the slightest degree of calligraphic freedom, activating and reworking his fruits with each subsequent stroke.

Demuth often used watercolor and graphite to depict fruits, vegetables, and flowers; such studies comprise a very rich part of his art. Besides the wide possibilities of color investigation that food permitted him, there is also its comparative neutrality as a subject: Few among us have very strong feelings about plums or eggplants, and they therefore provided the artist with a subject relatively unencumbered by symbolic or referential meaning. His watery rendering of eggplants and plums and the manner in which the plums appear to cascade upward out of the picture plane make them all seem to swell before us, as if a single sheet of paper cannot contain their abundant ripeness.

26

DORIS LEE

American (1905-1983)
Thanksgiving, 1935
Oil on canvas; 28⅛ x 40 in.
Mr. and Mrs. Frank G. Logan Prize Fund (1935.313)

There are not too many occasions more thoroughly American than Thanksgiving. Tied to colonial history, it is a national day of gratitude, centered around a feast symbolizing the joys and ties of family, speaking to generational continuity and the powerful meaning of home and hearth. Lee grew up in the small Illinois town of Aledo, and her paintings often hark back to the world of her youth. Tinged by the warm glow of memory, Lee's Aledo becomes almost a rural Arcadia, with the core values of America playing themselves out on domestic stages, full of charming, anecdotal incident.

In Lee's image of Thanksgiving, men are conspicuous by their absence. This is a world of women, sharing a kitchen abuzz with the activities involved in preparing a feast. Capturing hubbub with unerring accuracy, Lee created a tapestry of rich and sensitive observations. Her folksy style indelibly etched the individual personalities of her characters, right down to the dog contentedly warming itself beneath the stove. Children—including twins—watch and echo the frantic tempos of their elders. Like a Dutch genre painting, this scene becomes an almost anthropological record, a glimpse of a world fixed by the artist into an immutable moment of truth. The meal itself might mark the culmination of the holiday, but, clearly, for Lee, its true meaning lies in the ritual of its preparation.

27

GEORGES BRAQUE

French (1882-1963)
Still Life with Fruit and Stringed Instrument, 1938
Oil on canvas; 45 x 57¼ in.
Gift of Mary and Leigh Block (1988.141.6)

Still-life painting constitutes about three quarters of Georges Braque's entire *corpus* of work, a higher proportion than anyone in these pages since Chardin. The arrangement and rearrangement of objects in a studio setting fascinated Braque for almost sixty years. With his colleague Pablo Picasso, he used the genre to develop Cubism, and he employed it to center his thoughts about formal manipulation at every phase of his career.

This large painting is a superb example of Braque's aesthetic. Here he willfully jumbled visual sensations into overlapping pictorial fields, reinventing his sources into remnants of his encounter with them. Braque did not describe what he observed; rather, he attempted to re-create it, using pears, lemons, mandolins, tables, and the texture of paint as just the opening salvo for an assault on perception. Space, color, and optical verity become pictorial elements to be employed as Braque wished, made malleable and permutable to his will. Objects reverberate outside their contours, walls and floors collapse and realign, setting up turbulent rhythms that invest the composition with a dynamism curiously reminiscent of the work of Frans Synders (see plate 2). Braque tested the absolute edges of this dynamism, permitting it to come tantalizingly close to chaos, but rescued it with subtle acts of control—particularly in the employ of repeated areas of red, green, and lavender—that snatch a dizzying equilibrium from the jaws of anarchy.

28

Pierre Bonnard

French (1867-1947)
The Checkered Tablecloth, 1939
Oil on canvas; 23 x 23 in.
Gift of Mary and Leigh Block (1988.141.4)

Bonnard was seventy-two years old when he executed this painting, and it everywhere reflects the rich autumnal fruition of his very special and personal vision. Bonnard made color sing, as few were able to in the history of art; he could cause a basket of fruit on a table to appear incredibly voluptuous, creating a mood of intimacy so intense that it seems almost palpable. He saturated everything he touched with a kind of radiance, a tonal warmth and brilliance that embraces both subject and viewer. As an artist, he sought little more than that, and his stature rests in that he so regularly achieved his aims. The purely sensual fecundity these fruits exhibit is a bit reminiscent of Renoir's encounter with the light of the South, in his *Fruits from the Midi* (see plate 19).

For, from 1925 on, Bonnard lived in the south of France, near Cannes, in a house so modest that it provided him with only a very tiny studio. While many of his paintings from these years depict the artist's densely planted garden and the lush surrounding landscape, he also produced many compelling interiors. He would move from room to room, painting scenes in his kitchen, dining room, bath, and bedroom, instilling his work with a comfortable and domestic flavor. In this painting, a checkered dropcloth has been laid atop Bonnard's red-felt dining-room table cover, recognizable from its appearance in many of the artist's other canvases. His cramped quarters suited him perfectly; he made a virtue out of his need to present his scenes in close-up formats, tilting space toward the viewer to jam in more visual data. There is a kind of overwhelming ripeness at work here, a sureness of subject, handling, and pattern that is deceptively simple and extraordinarily pleasing.

29

IVAN LE LORRAIN ALBRIGHT

American (1897-1983)
Plattered Fish, Georgia, 1966
Gouache on paper; 16 x 20 in.
Gift of the artist (1977.260)

When Hollywood needed a painter in 1943 to execute the painting that would serve as the culminating moment in the filming of "The Portrait of Dorian Gray," they turned to Illinois native Ivan Albright. They knew that he, of all artists in the United States, could best depict the horrible ravages of a corrupt soul, render in paint the complete degradation of a man, and dramatically confront in oil the certain palpability of the wages of sin. Albright had always been attracted to what most would shun; during World War I, he was attached to the Medical Corps of the American Expeditionary Forces in France, where he made detailed drawings of field operations on the wounded, immersing himself in details of gore and viscera not as a sadist, but with an eye continually fascinated with the entire texture and panoply of life.

Albright brought this incessant urge to confront and overwhelm the senses to his occasional essays in still life. Here, he placed the viewer directly over a gilded tray bearing four swollen denizens of the deep, forcing a dialogue between consumer and consumed. There is no dill-flavored cream sauce, no light glazing of béchamel, not even some browned potatoes to ameliorate this curious confrontation. In a word, these fish stink. Like a moth to a flame, Albright was drawn toward his subject's predicament; he did several versions of this composition, and his palette seems to exaggerate the quality of their raw and decaying flesh. Nonetheless, he lovingly described their rather pathetic end. Albright's art can be at once coarse and revelatory, as it forces us to examine what is attractive and intriguing about what is repellent.

WAYNE THIEBAUD

American (born 1920)
Cakes No. 1, 1967
Pastel on tracing paper; 17½ x 18⅝ in.
Gift of the Society for Contemporary Art
(1971.391)

Thiebaud has always been an artist of sweet excess. His paintings, prints, and drawings of cakes, pies, candy, and hot dogs celebrate the special joys of conspicuous American consumerism. One could argue that Thiebaud revealed a good deal of what he thought life is about when he made a painting of a bowl of cherries in 1981; at any rate, his caloric onslaughts delight almost every sense and sensibility. Thiebaud knows what people want—they want more, and he is happy to give it to them.

Thiebaud surfaced from California at the same moment that the Pop artists were emerging in New York, and his art has often been linked with theirs. However, while Pop art is concerned with how mass culture is communicated through the media and with how things are packaged and made a part of social discourse, Thiebaud can actually be seen as much more of a traditional still-life artist. Little more than a charming amiability and a penchant for open-handed humor

separate Thiebaud from, say Juan Sánchez Cotán (see plate 1). Like the Spanish Baroque painter, he delights in the poetry of repeated shapes and in the potency of his medium to suggest the texture and taste of food. In this picture, he exulted in the pretty oval silhouettes made by his plethora of cakes, and in creating a surface of high-keyed colors that seems to be as sweet as the objects depicted. The high vantage point not only approximates the customer's experience with a store display, but also makes the composition more timeless, abstract, and evocative. Thiebaud gave each cake its own individual space in a tightly symmetrical composition in which six cakes seem to radiate around two smaller ones at the center. Looking like hats on stands, the cakes cast purplish shadows resembling lollipops. In this heightened fantasy of a bake-shop window, Thiebaud provided us with "user-friendly" art, creating an image that recognizes and touches the child within us all.

NOTES ABOUT THE AUTHOR

JAMES YOOD teaches art theory and criticism at Northwestern University and has taught art history at the School of The Art Institute of Chicago and Loyola University. He writes art criticism regularly for *Artforum* magazine and the *New Art Examiner*. His recent publications include the catalogue for the Refco Collection (Chicago and New York, 1990) and, with Patty Carroll, *Spirited Visions: Portraits of Chicago Artists* (University of Illinois Press, 1991).